MW01040776

OBSERVATIONS

From a Life Lived in Medicine

OBSERVATIONS

From a Life Lived in Medicine

Scott A. Kelly, M.D.

AHM
ART HEALS MEDIA

*One hundred percent of the profits of this book will go to fund
The Art Heals Media Foundation. The Art Heals Media Foundation
was created to lift the spirits of patients during trying times.*

ISBN 978-0-9912743-3-8 (hardcover)
ISBN 978-0-9912743-1-4 (paperback)
ISBN 978-0-9912743-5-2 (audiobook)

Cover design by Laura Duffy
Book design by Karen Minster
Images © / Adobe Stock

Printed in the United States of America

First Printing, 2022

Art Heals Media, Inc.
553 Peachtree Battle Avenue
Atlanta, GA 30305

For my muses—
Caelyn, Elizabeth, and Deborah.

What a beautiful life we have created together.

A Note from the Author

I spent my formative years in a classroom. The education of becoming a physician requires it—countless hours amongst the backdrop of green chalkboards, uncomfortable wooden desks, and smells of glue and chalk dust. I often stared out the window, wishing I were somewhere else. My studies were long on theory but short on practicality. Real life turned out to be quite different and bore little resemblance to what I'd imagined.

My actual education in becoming a physician began when I left the classroom. The most incandescent memories of my life took place within an inner-city hospital while training to become a physician. The noises and smells became familiar: the beeping of a heart rhythm dancing across a telemetry monitor, the waves of smells of sickness, and the gentle undertones of groans interrupted by occasional violent screams of family members when they lost those they love. The long hours at my patients' bedside taught me about the human spirit's challenges and resilience. These experiences cut me deep. I was thrown into the fire and had the scars and the hard knots of human experience to prove it. They remain with me to this day.

During my life in medicine, I learned the fragility and unpredictability of the human condition—brief glimpses into the infallible logic that reminds us that we are all temporary. My experience gave me an intimate view of humanity's best and worst: a constant revolving door of human challenges and triumph. My time spent there taught me that we all have the undercurrent of time ticking within us. If we listen hard enough, it's there. It serves us all well to listen.

I realize that all of the experiences have woven themselves into my character's fabric. The experiences lit a fuse in me that continues to burn: an indelible mark on who I am currently and how I will strive to live the rest of my time on this earth. These experiences left me with an incessant desire to become a better version of myself.

I learned more from the practice of medicine than I ever did in the classroom. I took notes. Medicine is as much about the heart as it is about the mind. These are my observations of the human condition from a life lived in medicine.

OBSERVATIONS

From a Life Lived in Medicine

I've learned that moments best measure the cadence of life.

I've learned that life is a kaleidoscope of emotions—
love, pain, loss, fear, hope, and love. Sometimes it is best to
sit back and revel in amazement at the brilliant colors.

I've learned it is always best to garner respect with a depth
of character rather than business acumen.

I've learned
that happiness
is about random
collisions—and
how you deal
with them.

I've learned it is essential to hone the mind, for it will remain malleable. Keep evolving until you take your last breath. It is more than the process of becoming intelligent and wiser. Be comfortable in your skin—confident without insecurities. Know who you are without being dependent on what others think of you.

I've learned that life is a constant struggle between the resolution of temporary pleasure and happiness.

I've learned that being genuine is doing and saying what you believe.

I've learned it is best to study yourself to find your weakness and obtain a well-limned view of your strengths and magnify them. It is hard to progress forward without that simple understanding.

SCOTT A. KELLY, M.D.

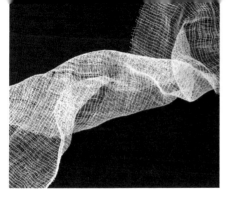

I've learned that time does not heal all wounds. They become tolerable and sometimes advantageous if we learn to accept and embrace them.

I've learned it is always best to be graceful and commanding. The real trick is to figure out how to do both simultaneously.

I've learned that confidence without clarity of vision is as dangerous as ignorance.

I've learned to embrace the ocean of difference between being alone or being lonely.

I've learned that happiness in life inherently depends on your ability to filter out the noise.

I've learned it is best to hurl yourself into the world with
the hope of being caught but to have the common sense to
create your net if the timing is off.

I've learned that there is a difference between emotional scars
and physical scars. The emotional scars are worse.

I've learned that
unconditional love
evolves out of consistency.
It is not the intensity of
a one-time event; it is
the daily, loving acts that
make the difference.

I've learned it is always best to surround yourself with people
that bring out the best in you.

I've learned that life is a bewildering array of emotions.
It is best to keep those emotions in check.

I've learned there is great comfort in shared grief.

I've learned that even the most brilliant lives have their share of injudicious moments.

I've learned the immutable truth that taking an inventory of gratitude daily will always serve you well.

I've learned to appreciate the beauty of a sound mind and a functioning body.

I've learned that the vicissitudes of daily life stand little chance to an unwavering belief of the subconscious mind in a different outcome.

I've learned that many people often spend their entire adult life repairing the damage done to them in childhood.

I've learned it is best to go through life with an unflinching search for the truth and honesty, especially when trying to understand yourself.

I've learned that the ability to turn off the desire for external validation is integral to the pursuit of happiness.

I've learned never to underestimate outside pressures on a relationship. It is best to keep those external pressures in check.

I've learned that the best way to get out of the fog of grief is to press on.

I've learned it is best to accept total and personal responsibility for your life's outcome and refrain from the constant search for external validation.

I've learned it is natural to evince bitterness and distrust if the adults in your life didn't love and protect you while you were young. I was one of the lucky ones who benefitted from loving parents.

I've learned that always waiting for the perfect time carries the inherent risk of believing the grand assumption that time is guaranteed.

I've learned it is a constant struggle for the human condition to lean away from an existence plagued by self-doubt and insecurity.

I've learned
that those willing
to choose an alternate
path in life, away
from superficiality
to embrace the human
spirit's levity and
depth, live more
meaningful lives.

I've learned that the best way to have friends is to develop
a genuine and honest interest in others. If you love them,
they will love you in return.

I've learned that those whose lives
are filled with a bouquet of remarkable
experiences will love, serve others,
and create the foundation of their life
based on gratitude. They are bright
and shining stars in the darkness of
an unforgiving and often inhumane
world. They have chosen their path.
The rest of the world chooses to
live differently.

I've learned that you will have friends who repeatedly
choose the right decision and those that don't. It is important
to celebrate their success and lift them from their missteps
and misfortunes.

I've learned there is no downside to weaving kindness, love, and empathy into your character.

I've learned it is hard not to turn to nostalgia for an irrecoverable past when your life takes a turn for the worst.

I've learned it is always best to take a clear-eyed and honest look at yourself. You will find that you are the common denominator in all of your challenges in life. And you are also the catalyst for the resolution.

I've learned human perception is often misguided. When in doubt, rely on scientific facts.

I've learned it is best to build a reservoir of life experiences. You will need these life experiences to lean on in times of challenge.

I've learned
the surest way to
advance the human
condition is with
unhuman discipline,
compassion,
and grace.

I've learned only to do things that try to serve you well.
Live a life that is honest, genuine, and real. Whether performed
on others or self-sabotaging, every malicious act has a
downstream effect on the heart and mind. Life is rarely black
or white. There are always various gray shades of moral clarity.

I've learned that life has a way of taking you to the edge and
back, but you might find it of great comfort that you are not
alone. Many people have traversed the same road before
you and found a solution. Although the situation feels unique
to you, simply because it is your problem at the time, I can
assure you that it is not. Human vulnerability is a universal
experience.

I've learned to appreciate mindless tranquility where thoughts are absent and peace and serenity are abundant. It is difficult to be depressed, angry, or feel pain in the absence of thought and internal conflict.

I've learned that life is about the occasional moment of radiance, filtered by the times of feeling nothing or being miserable.

I've learned that if you find the work you love, surround yourself with people that inspire you, and fill your time with activities that you enjoy—then count yourself among the elite. Be content and appreciative.

I've learned that the best way to fight life's battles is from within. The trick is to arise from the rubble tattered but with our spirit intact. The actual change is more than continental drift. It is more like a tectonic shift among one's soul.

I've learned there is some measure of sacrifice in all outstanding accomplishments.

I've learned that the best way to guarantee success is daily and consistent action with unrelenting discipline. Favorable outcomes are rarely a random stroke of luck. An inner vision of hope and brilliance is inherently dependent on consistent, purposeful acts. The secret to success is no secret. It is pressing forward with unbridled passion, unwavering consistency, and iron focus while leveraging subconscious thought.

I've learned it is far too easy to lean toward mediocrity. Push yourself.

I've learned that intense pain and dissatisfaction with one's current state of being is the underpinning of significant transformation. Without the pain, most transformations are temporary. Violent tides of change are more likely to occur in times of despair.

I've learned misplaced optimism serves us better than misplaced pessimism.

I've learned never to underestimate the power of discipline. Discipline is the lighthouse to help you navigate and find your bearings in a turbulent world. Living a life without discipline is a guaranteed life of internal conflict. The difference between muddling through the world and living a life on solid footing

is a clear vision in the subconscious mind. When you begin to live a more disciplined life, you will notice an uptick in happiness— a profound sense of worth and validation.

I've learned that one of the challenges of the human condition is always to try to attribute our minds toward mindless entities that we cannot control despite our best efforts. We long for human control over things that aren't controllable. It is sobering to find out that you have less control of life in front of you than we had hoped. That said, it does not excuse you from using common sense and sound judgment to improve the odds.

I've learned currents of emotion run like tides, and it is always best to keep a watchful eye on those tides so you don't get surprised by an undertow.

I've learned that if you find yourself in a relationship with integrity, respect, and friendship—hold on to it. You've found something special. Love adds levity and depth to the human spirit.

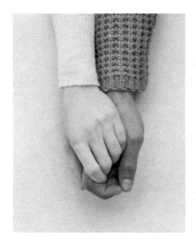

SCOTT A. KELLY, M.D.

I've learned that overcoming a challenging upbringing has one reoccurring theme—the absolute refusal to let irresponsible parents define them. They do not accept that abuse is generational. They refuse to let their childhood atrocities evolve into recycled pain for those they choose to bring into the world and love.

I've learned it is a very precarious situation to search for a life of enlightenment while continually trying to live up to others' expectations.

I've learned there are times that I feel the invincible need to escape into myself. I've come to terms with that.

I've learned that the only thing that can heal a damaged soul from the battlefield of life experiences is love.

I've learned never to underestimate the power of disciplined human potential.

I've learned that sometimes people just don't cry for help. An unburdened face does not mean one is not free of worry and silently suffering.

I've learned your occupation will consume a large part of your life. Never settle. Do something that inspires you daily.

I've learned that a penchant for drugs and alcohol will never solve a state of disillusionment propelled by a fractured marriage, a strained relationship with children, or a career headed off the cliffs. They will temporarily numb and quiet the chaotic thoughts in our minds but limit the joy. Drugs and alcohol don't ease a mind flooded with thoughts and despair: they drown it out. They will numb your joy far more than your pain and create collateral damage to all the relationships around you. It is a holocaust of one's soul in slow motion.

I've learned it is best to lean away from the accumulation and lean toward a reductionist frame of mind. It is best to live a life centered on appreciation rather than an insatiable desire for materialism. The constant pursuit of temporary pleasure objects is incompatible with enlightenment— labels obscure objectivity. The human condition is a world of contrasts: the simple life versus materialism and simplicity versus abundance. I find it particularly appealing in an individual to have an abundance of resources without a penchant for unfulfilled wanting. The pursuit of objects pales in comparison to relationships and meaningful experiences.

I've learned solitude in small doses can help one's soul, but never underestimate companionship. We are pack animals. A lack of friendship can make one's soul wither.

I've learned that the manifold struggles of striving to become an authentic individual rarely outweigh the pleasure of achieving the outcome.

I've learned it is best to steer clear of people who prefer humiliating others to ease the burden of hiding the pain of their insecurities. Others' temporary opinions should never bleed into how you feel about yourself. Your internal moral compass should be the barometer for your character's gauge. People have a right to their opinion, and you have an equal right not to accept their opinion—particularly when their idea is of you. I've learned that the advice of others, despite their best intentions, will rarely measure up to your intuition.

I've learned that we have difficulty understanding abstract and intangible things, so we try to put a human face to it. It is the only way we can begin to understand. We try to simplify, but we complicate.

I've learned that achieving vaulting ambition results from cultivating others' talents. Life is a team sport. Be the visionary and captain of your team.

I've learned that actions and decisions carry weight. It is easy to be conflicted—because of a need for self-preservation but reverence for humanity. A blur of poor judgment can forever change lives. The choices we make in life are pretty simple, either the inconvenience of discipline or the pain of regret. People rationalize pleasure and obey pain. Life is more palatable with a clear mind and total consciousness.

I've learned that the weight of a loss can burden people throughout the remainder of their lives on earth. The gravity of a situation can unravel their world. It is best to reach out to them and lift them up.

I've learned that we all want godsends, but be sure to pay attention to the little gifts.

I've learned that training the subconscious mind is the key to outstanding achievement in our limited time on earth. Never underestimate the power of the subconscious mind to deliver reality. Those that have tapped into greatness believed it with every ounce of their soul's core before it happened. The subconscious mind doesn't know the difference between a real or a vividly and intently imagined event.

I've learned sometimes we know better, but we do the opposite.

I've learned that the subconscious mind's attic is littered with many treasures, and we all have latent talents that are undiscovered.

I've learned that life can change on a dime. One second your life can be moving along brilliantly and then suddenly be derailed. Brace yourself for the unknown and forge ahead.

I've learned it is easy to veer away from your authentic core, your spirit, yourself. The world around you will lure you from your true self—don't let it. You do have a choice.

I've learned to pay great attention to how others treat those that cannot do anything for them. It says everything about their character and their heart—and whether I want them in my life or not.

I've learned that sometimes you will feel hopeless, and sometimes you will feel hope. The real difference in living a remarkable life is to feel hope most of the time.

I've learned that natural talent comes out of the shadows in the most unforeseen ways.

I've learned that personal decency, character, authenticity, and discipline can make a simple person stand tall, a giant among us. Those with astonishing power and presence do not look outside of themselves for validation. Everything they need is within them.

I've learned that clearing the thoughts in your mind can produce calm in the sea of turbulence and uncertainty. This calm creates an oasis in a world that is brimming with doom and despair. A wandering mind can lead to unhappiness if not kept in check.

I've learned I'm not exactly sure what enlightenment is, but I believe it is close to this: Living life in a constant state of meditation, with an absence of thought but retaining a subconscious clarity of purpose. A life filled to the brim with gratitude. A place of deep peace and contentment.

I've learned that the world is full of comets soaring and crashing. The real trick is to realize you are the comet. Write your treatise, or someone will write it for you without your consent. Break out of the gilded cage.

I've learned that life will weigh you down until your burdens are overwhelming The only way to defy gravity and bounce around without any concerns or worries is to decide who you want to be and become that person.

I've learned the importance of setting personal boundaries.

I've learned moments of clarity do occur in perfect storms, and the silver lining in a dark cloud is never as far away as one thinks.

I've learned inspiration is easier to find if your eyes and heart are open.

I've learned no one lives a life of sustained brilliance. Even the most respected and brightest people will have their moment of episodic stupidity.

I've learned it is much better to live an itinerant life than remain stagnant in an unfulfilled life.

I've learned that the concept of neuroplasticity of the brain is correct. One can evolve and improve life by consistent retraining of the subconscious mind.

I've learned the best-lived life is one in pursuit of rich experiences and not just living to avoid suffering.

I've learned that the outcome of weathered pain is a high tolerance for discomfort.

I've learned if you have love and gratitude, you don't need much else.

I've learned to confront adversity head-on, embracing different viewpoints and trusting intuition to make the right call. Seldom do problems go away without the first step of acknowledgment.

I've learned some people have an incessant tilt toward a path of self-destruction and they spend their lives fighting this. The human condition can fray the fortitude of the strongest souls.

I've learned it is best to live a contemplative and meditative life.

I've learned we are all living in a world of finite mortality. Some choose to acknowledge this more than others. Perhaps this is

why we live in various shades of enlightenment at any given time. We are all fallible individuals living on borrowed time, and we are all searching to fill the empty void within our souls. It is never too early to begin the self-awareness journey; it's never too late either.

I've learned to be wary of those with a morbid curiosity disguised as empathy.

I've learned it is best to live fully, regardless of the outcome.

I've learned that if you dare to create a new world for yourself since the other didn't quite fulfill you, there is no need to ask others for permission to live in it.

I've learned it is best to find some order in our chaotic existence. Whether it is through discipline, meditation, or religion—it is paramount to find that structure.

I've learned that
the mind is a garden.
It is best to cultivate it,
nourish it, protect it.

I've learned that the power of a health crisis forces you to venture off into unfamiliar territory and reevaluate everything in your life. It makes you realize that you can become more alive as you move closer to death.

I've learned the universe will create challenges for you daily. Sometimes it is best to walk right through the wall rather than to find a way around it.

I've learned that others universally admire the people who walk their own path in life. They walk on the edge of life without the worry of being defeated. They rely on counter-intuitive thought. We admire them because we silently wish we dared to do the same.

I've learned that the best way to help others going through trying times is to lean away from saccharine sentiments or explain away the event with a reason. Comfort comes from your presence and your willingness to listen. Let them navigate their way through their challenge.

I've learned that the quality of life can prove to be more important than longevity. Sometimes advances in technology and heroic measures are not always in our own best interest.

I've learned sudden and tragic loss affects each of us differently. For some, it is a bump in the road, and for others, the wound is calamitous. Loss can dull creativity, sharpen anger, and make one resent everything they previously valued. Do not let events define you—no matter how painful they appear to be.

I've learned that life is a beautiful mess: complicated, challenging, and thrilling. Some days will seem like a lifetime. Other days are fleeting.

I've learned that those with thorny attitudes deserve to spend a lot of time alone.

I've learned it is best to weather insults and criticism with a chin held high and a steadfast heart.

I've learned there are very few things in life as pleasurable as the thrill of a rekindled relationship.

I've learned that life is a long conversation, and it is always best to make it a good one.

I've learned that overcoming lamentable moments is achieved by the satisfaction of pursuing and doing something well.

I've learned it is always best to complete the actions you least want to do first. Get them out of the way so you can enjoy the rest of your morning, your afternoon, your evening, and your life.

I've learned that risk is a part of life. The difference is calculating the vacuous risks from the intelligent ones and having the awareness and courage to pivot as the situation's direction evolves.

I've learned education can only take you so far. Education is simply a foundation of knowledge. You must rely on creativity and explore counterintuitive thought at some time in your life. Do not let your education define you. Cultivate your unique thoughts.

I've learned to have a special ire for fabrication and a particular disdain for drama. Life itself is challenging enough without fueling uncertainty and creating problems that do not exist.

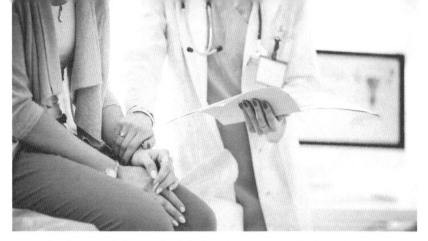

I've learned that a physician's role is not to calculate the value of one particular life but to determine all human life as invaluable. And the best way to improve a doctor–patient relationship is to limit the people between a doctor and a patient.

I've learned never to let your desire for pleasure or success outpace your moral compass.

I've learned that life is continuously changing. As we look down the long corridor of life, there will be times in life when we will cringe and retreat into ourselves. And that is acceptable. Let it go. Choose your battles wisely because there will be times in life where you will need to soldier on. And you will need every ounce of strength to do so.

I've learned the most heartwarming moments occur at the most unexpected times.

I've learned most people at their soul's core are well-meaning. They are lured off the path of a well-lived life by observing others who lead an undisciplined life. They become bent toward temporary pleasures to escape the pain. They muddle through the world rather than living a life on solid footing. It is a slippery slope.

I've learned accolades and trophies are a poor reflection of a well-lived life. A collection of great moments is a more accurate barometer.

I've learned when the heart and mind are aligned, the word *impossible* doesn't exist.

I've learned that the removal of things, rather than addition, will often bring us closer to happiness.

I've learned how important it is to continue evolving and growing. I'm finding myself less interested in small talk and even less interested in sharing my time with people who don't have my back.

I've learned it is impossible to slalom through life without regrets and remorse. The trick is not to stay in those moments too long.

I've learned relationships often fray, not because of a lack of love but because of outside pressures. It is best to eliminate those external pressures.

I've learned it is best to have a clear view of where you want to be in the future and then turn it over to your subconscious mind. There is no need to dwell on it. Let go and trust in your subconscious mind to deliver. It will provide a clear path.

I've learned that choosing a career is one of the most important decisions you will make. Choose wisely. It will demand a large part of your life on this earth. Never settle for something that doesn't inspire you.

I've learned that we develop into the summation of our experiences and the total of the people we meet. Never underestimate the entrance of others into your life.

I've learned that your alchemy hinges upon your ability to accept personal responsibility. Don't wait for a flash of brilliance or the luminous advice of another person: create

your own world. You will become venerated and beloved by others without seeking their approval. They have no choice but to applaud you even if the applause is silent.

I've learned it is a part of the human condition to eagerly hand over others' responsibility for our happiness, our pleasure, and often our hopes and dreams. I've learned not to let others' opinions drown out your voice. Nods of approvals from others provide temporary pleasure, but they won't sustain you. Curate your own life.

I've learned to find great comfort in the fact that many have survived historical atrocity and individual despair, only to come out stronger on the other side.

As I reflect upon my years in medicine, I realize that my classroom time was significant. It gave me the foundation to understand the intricacies of the human body's anatomy and physiology. It taught me how to alleviate suffering and pain. It taught me how to eliminate the disease. But it was only a small, but vital, component on the road to becoming a physician. The most valuable part of my education took place in the eye of the storm of dealing with the human condition. The experience was revelatory, profoundly moving, and illuminated the wonderful and beautiful shared moments that occur when people share a common vision of helping each other. For that, I am forever grateful.